100

things you should know about

PREHISTORIC LIFE

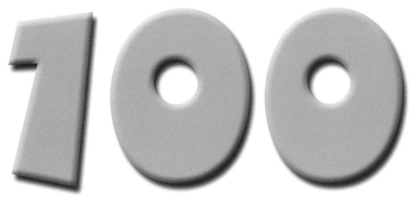

100
things you should know about
PREHISTORIC LIFE

Rupert Matthews
Consultant: Steve Parker

MiLes
KeLLy
PUBLISHING

First published in 2006 by Miles Kelly Publishing Ltd
Bardfield Centre, Great Bardfield, Essex, CM7 4SL

2 4 6 8 10 9 7 5 3 1

Editorial Director: Belinda Gallagher
Art Director: Jo Brewer
Volume Designers: Sophie Pelham, Tom Slemmings
Indexer: Jane Parker
Production: Elizabeth Brunwin
Reprographics: Anthony Cambray,
Mike Coupe, Ian Paulyn

ISBN 1-84236-643-2

Printed in China

British Library Cataloguing-in-Publication Data
A catalogue record for this book is available from the British Library

ACKNOWLEDGEMENTS
The publishers would like to thank the following
artists who have contributed to this book:
Martin Camm, Mark Davis/Mackerel,
Peter Dennis/Linda Rogers Associates,
Mike Foster/Maltings Partnership, Andrea Morandi,
Bob Nicholls, Steve Roberts, Eric Rowe/Linden Artists,
Mike Saunders, Rudi Vizi, Mike White/Temple Rogers

www.mileskelly.net
info@mileskelly.net

Contents

Long, long ago

1 **The Earth was once covered by huge sheets of ice.** This happened several times during Earth's history and we call these frozen times ice ages. However, the ice ages are a tiny part of prehistory. Before then, the world was warm and lakes and seas covered the land. Even earlier than this, there was little rain for thousands of years, and the land was covered in deserts. Over millions of years, weather and conditions changed. Living things changed too, in order to survive. This change is called 'evolution'.

Woolly rhinoceros

Cave lion

Mammoth tusks are sometimes caught by fishermen in the North Sea, which was dry land during the ice age.

▼ A scene from the last ice age, about 10,000 years ago. Animals grew thick fur coats to protect themselves from the cold. Many animals, such as woolly mammoths, survived on plants such as mosses. Others, such as cave lions, were fierce hunters, needing meat to survive.

Aurochs

Woolly mammoth

Megaloceros

Life begins

2 **Life began a very, very long time ago.** We know this from the remains of prehistoric life forms that died and were buried. Over millions of years, their remains turned into shapes in rocks, called fossils. The first fossils are over 3000 million years old. They are tiny 'blobs' called bacteria – living things that still survive today.

3 **The first plants were seaweeds, which appeared about 1000 million years ago.** Unlike bacteria and blue-green algae, which each had just one living cell, these plants had thousands of cells. Some seaweeds were many metres long. They were called algae – the same name that scientists use today.

4 **By about 800 million years ago, some plants were starting to grow on land.** They were mixed with other living things called moulds, or fungi. Together, the algae (plants) and fungi formed flat green-and-yellow crusts that crept over rocks and soaked up rain. They were called lichens. These still grow on rocks and trees today.

▼ Fossils of *Anomalocaris* have been found in Canada. It had a circular mouth and finlike body parts. Its body was covered by a shell.

5 **The first animals lived in the sea – and they were as soft as jelly!** Over 600 million years ago, some of the first animals were jellyfish, floating in the water. On the seabed lived groups of soft, feathery-looking creatures called *Charnia*. This animal was an early type of coral. Animals need to take in food by eating other living things. *Charnia* caught tiny plants in its 'feathers'.

Jellyfish

Charnia

◀ *Charnia* looked like a prehistoric plant, but it was actually an animal!

6 **One of the first hunting animals was *Anomalocaris*.** It lived 520 million years ago, swimming through the sea in search of prey. It caught smaller creatures in its pincers, then pushed them into its mouth. *Anomalocaris* was a cousin of crabs and insects. It was one of the biggest hunting animals of its time, even though it was only 60 centimetres long.

▲ The *Cooksonia* plant had forked stems that carried water. The earliest examples have been found in Ireland.

7 **By 400 million years ago, plants on land were growing taller.** They had stiff stems that held them upright and carried water to their topmost parts. An early upright plant was *Cooksonia*. It was the tallest living thing on land, yet it was only 5 centimetres high – hardly the size of your thumb!

Animals swarm the seas

8 **Some of the first common animals were worms.** However, they were not earthworms in soil. At the time there was no soil and the land was bare. These worms lived in the sea. They burrowed in mud for plants and animals to eat.

◄ *Ottoia* was a sea worm that fed by filtering tiny food particles from the sea.

▼ Trilobites moved quickly across the seabed. Some could roll up into a ball like woodlice do today. This was a means of protection.

9 **The next animals to become common were trilobites.** They first lived about 550 million years ago in the sea. Trilobites crawled along the seabed eating tiny bits of food they found. Their name means 'three lobes' (parts). A trilobite had two grooves along its back, from head to tail, so its body had three main parts – left, middle and centre.

▼ *Pterygotus* was a fierce hunter, with large eyes and long claws.

10 **Trilobites were some of the first animals with legs that bent at the joints.** Animals with jointed legs are called arthropods. They have been the most common creatures for millions of years, including trilobites long ago, and later on, crabs, spiders and insects. Like other arthropods, trilobites had a tough, outer shell for protection.

11 **Some of the first hunters were sea scorpions – some were as big as lions!** *Pterygotus* was 2 metres long. It swished its tail to chase prey through water, which it tore apart with its huge claws. Sea scorpions lived 500 to 250 million years ago. Unlike modern scorpions, they had no sting in their tails.

12

For millions of years the seabed was covered with the curly shells of ammonites. Some of these shells were as small as your fingernail, others were bigger than dinner plates. Ammonites were successful creatures and thousands of kinds survived for millions of years. Each ammonite had big eyes to see prey and long tentacles (arms) to catch it with. Ammonites died out at the same time as the dinosaurs, around 65 million years ago.

▼ *Pikaia* looked a little bit like an eel with fins.

▲ This rock contains an ammonite fossil. The shell would have protected the soft-bodied creature inside.

13

Among the worms, trilobites and ammonites was a small creature that had a very special body part – the beginnings of a backbone. It was called *Pikaia* and lived about 530 million years ago. Gradually, more animals with backbones, called vertebrates, evolved from it. Today, vertebrates rule much of the world – they are fish, reptiles, birds and mammals.

QUIZ

1. Did sea scorpions have stings in their tails?
2. What does the name 'trilobite' mean?
3. What kind of animal was *Ottoia*?
4. When did ammonites die out?
5. What was special about *Pikaia*?

Answers:
1. No 2. Three lobes, or parts
3. A worm 4. 65 million years ago
5. It had an early type of backbone

Very fishy

14 **The first fish could not bite – they were suckers!** About 500 million years ago, new animals appeared in the sea – the first fish. They had no jaws or teeth and probably sucked in worms and small pieces of food from the mud.

▲ *Hemicyclaspis* was an early jawless fish. It had eyes on top of its head and probably lived on the seabed. This way it could keep a look out for predators above.

15 **Some early fish wore suits of armour!** They had hard, curved plates of bone all over their bodies for protection. These fish were called placoderms and most were fierce hunters. Some had huge jaws with sharp sheets of bone for slicing up prey.

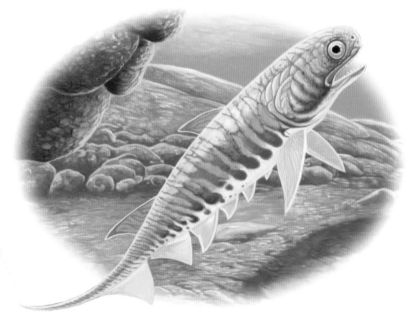

16 **Spiny sharks had spines, but they were not really sharks.** These fish were similar in shape to today's sharks, but they lived in rivers and lakes, not the sea, about 430 million years ago. *Climatius* was a spiny shark that looked fierce, but it was only as big as your finger!

◀ The fins on the back of *Climatius* were supported by needle–sharp spines. These helped to protect it from attacks by squid or other fish.

17 The first really big hunting fish was bigger than today's great white shark! *Dunkleosteus* grew to almost 10 metres long and swam in the oceans 360 million years ago. It sliced up prey, such as other fish, using its massive teeth made of narrow blades of bone, each one as big as this book.

18 Some early fish started to 'walk' out of water. Types of fish called lobefins appeared 390 million years ago. Their side fins each had a 'stump' at the base made of muscle. If the water in their pool dried up, lobefins could use their fins like stubby legs to waddle over land to another pool. *Eusthenopteron* was a lobefin fish about 1.2 metres long. Over millions of years, some lobefins evolved into four-legged animals called tetrapods.

VERY FISHY!
You will need:
waxed card (like the kind used to make milk cartons) crayons scissors piece of soap

Place the piece of waxed card face down. Fold the card up at the edges. Draw a fish on the card. Cut a small notch in the rear of the card and wedge the piece of soap in it. Put the 'fish' in a bath of cold water and watch it swim away.

◄ *Eusthenopteron* could clamber about on dry land when moving from one stretch of water to another.

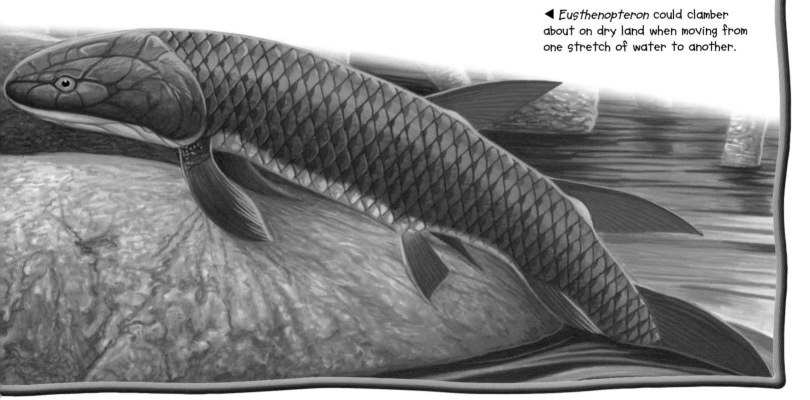

Animals invade the land

19 **The first land animals lived about 450 million years ago.** These early creatures, which came from the sea, were arthropods – creatures with hard outer body casings and jointed legs. They included prehistoric insects, spiders and millipedes. *Arthropleura* was a millipede – it was 2 metres in length!

▶ *Arthropleura* was as long as a human and was the largest–ever land arthropod.

20 **Some amphibians were fierce hunters.** *Gerrothorax* was about one metre long and spent most of its time at the bottom of ponds or streams. Its eyes pointed upward, to see fish swimming past, just above. *Gerrothorax* would then jump up to grab the fish in its wide jaws.

21 **The first four-legged animal had eight toes on each front foot!** *Acanthostega* used its toes to grip water plants as it swam. It lived about 380 million years ago and was one metre long. Creatures like it soon began to walk on land, too. They were called tetrapods, which means 'four legs'. They were a big advance in evolution – the first land animals with backbones.

◀ *Acanthostega* probably spent most of its time in water. It had gills for breathing underwater as well as lungs for breathing air.

23

Soon four–legged animals called amphibians were racing across the land. Amphibians were the first backboned animals to move fast out of the water. *Aphaneramma* had long legs and could run quickly. However, prehistoric amphibians, like those of today such as frogs and newts, had to return to the water to lay their eggs.

22

Fins became legs for walking on land, and tails changed, too. As the fins of lobefin fish evolved into legs, their tails became longer and more muscular. *Ichthyostega* had a long tail with a fin along its upper side. This tail design was good for swimming in water, and also helpful when wriggling across a swamp.

24

Some amphibians grew as big as crocodiles! *Eogyrinus* was almost 5 metres long and had strong jaws and teeth, like a crocodile. However, it lived about 300 million years ago, long before any crocodiles appeared. Although *Eogyrinus* could walk on dry land, it spent most of its time in streams and swamps.

◀ *Ichthyostega* had short legs, so it could probably only move slowly on land.

Life after death

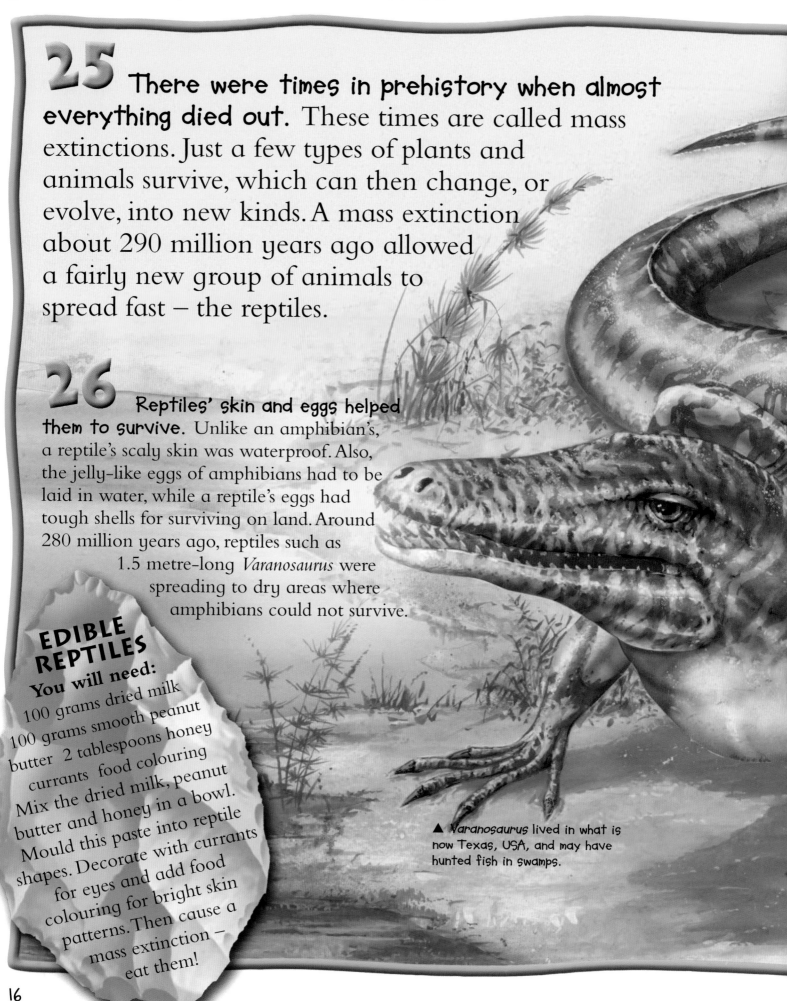

25 There were times in prehistory when almost everything died out. These times are called mass extinctions. Just a few types of plants and animals survive, which can then change, or evolve, into new kinds. A mass extinction about 290 million years ago allowed a fairly new group of animals to spread fast – the reptiles.

26 Reptiles' skin and eggs helped them to survive. Unlike an amphibian's, a reptile's scaly skin was waterproof. Also, the jelly-like eggs of amphibians had to be laid in water, while a reptile's eggs had tough shells for surviving on land. Around 280 million years ago, reptiles such as 1.5 metre-long *Varanosaurus* were spreading to dry areas where amphibians could not survive.

EDIBLE REPTILES

You will need:
100 grams dried milk
100 grams smooth peanut
butter 2 tablespoons honey
currants food colouring
Mix the dried milk, peanut
butter and honey in a bowl.
Mould this paste into reptile
shapes. Decorate with currants
for eyes and add food
colouring for bright skin
patterns. Then cause a
mass extinction –
eat them!

▲ *Varanosaurus* lived in what is now Texas, USA, and may have hunted fish in swamps.

Early reptiles had skulls made up of solid plates of bone. This made their heads strong, but heavy.

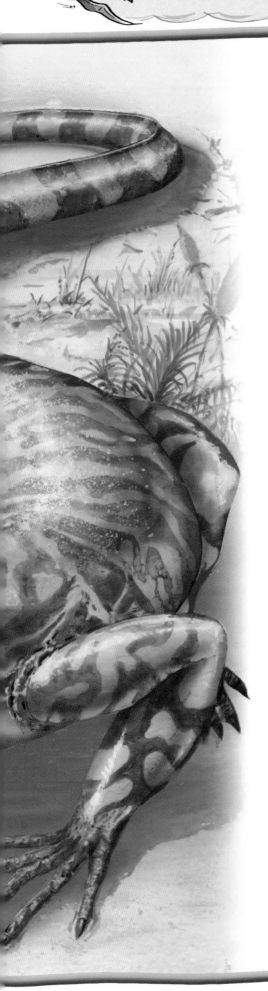

▶ *Hylonomus* lived in forests in what is now Canada. It hunted insects, spiders and millipedes.

27 **The first reptile looked like a lizard.** However *Hylonomus* belonged to a different reptile group to lizards. It lived like a lizard, chasing prey on the ground and in trees. It lived 345 million years ago.

28 **Some reptiles started to avoid bad weather by sleeping underground.** *Diictodon* lived about 260 million years ago and used its large teeth to chop up tough plant food. It may have dug holes to shelter from the heat, cold and rain.

▲ *Diictodon* had strong legs and sharp claws for burrowing.

Wars around the world

▼ The nostrils and eyes of *Mastodonsaurus* were on top of its head so that it could breathe and look around whilst hiding underwater.

29 **Some amphibians fought back against the reptiles.** *Mastodonsaurus* was a big, strong amphibian, 2 metres long, with sharp teeth. It hunted fish, other amphibians, and small reptiles. It lived at a time when reptiles were spreading even faster, about 250 to 203 million years ago. But most other big amphibians did not survive the reptiles.

30 **Other amphibians managed to survive the reptile takeover, too.** They were mainly small and hid in water or swamps. One was *Branchiosaurus*, which was about 12 centimetres long and hunted small fish in ponds.

▲ *Lystrosaurus* lived in Antarctica when it was a land of lush, tropical plant life. Today it is a frozen continent, covered by thick ice.

I DON'T BELIEVE IT!

Mastodonsaurus may have had tusks sticking out of its nose! Two front teeth may have poked through holes at the end of its snout.

31

Reptiles showed how the world's lands moved about. *Lystrosaurus* lived about 200 million years ago and its fossils come from Europe, Asia, Africa and Antarctica. This reptile could not swim, so all of these landmasses, or continents, must have been joined together at one time. Over millions of years, they drifted apart to form today's positions.

▼ As well as sharp teeth, *Moschops* had very strong skull bones, so it may have head-butted rivals in fights.

32

Some plant-eating reptiles had very sharp teeth. *Moschops* was as big as a rhino and lived in southern Africa about 270 million years ago. Its teeth were long and straight, and ended with a sharp edge like a chisel. *Moschops* could easily bite tough leaves and twigs off bushes.

Reptiles take over

33 Reptiles don't like to be too hot, or too cold. Otherwise they may overheat, or be too cold to move. Most reptiles bask in sunshine to get warm, then stay in the shade. *Dimetrodon* was a fierce reptile. It had a large 'sail' of skin on its back to soak up heat from the sun.

▲ The name *Dimetrodon* means 'two-types-of-teeth'. It was given this name as it had stabbing teeth and slicing teeth. It measured 3 metres in length.

QUIZ

1. How did *Dimetrodon* get warm?
2. Which types of reptile evolved into mammals?
3. How did some early reptiles swim?
4. Did the first crocodiles like water?

Answers:
1. By basking in the sun
2. Therapsids 3. By swishing their tails from side to side 4. No, they hated it!

34 The first crocodiles hated water! An early type of crocodile, *Protosuchus*, stayed on land. It lived in North America about 190 million years ago. It was one metre long and could run across dry land when hunting, using its long legs.

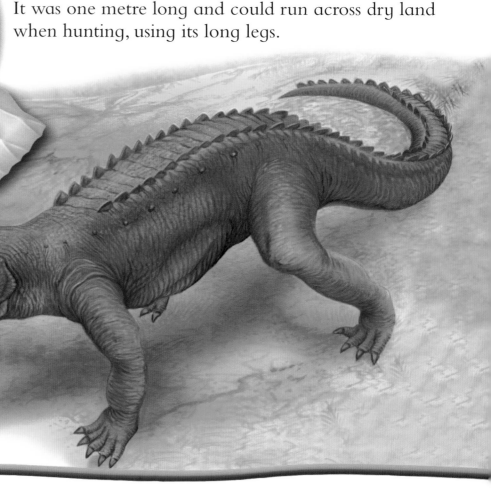

▶ *Protosuchus* had very powerful jaw muscles to snap its teeth shut on prey.

▶ *Chasmatosaurus* had teeth on the roof of its mouth as well as in its jaws.

35 **Some reptiles moved by using their tails.** Many types of early reptiles had long, strong tails. They probably lived in water and swished their tails to push themselves along. *Chasmatosaurus* was 2 metres long and probably hunted for fish. It looked like a crocodile but was more closely related to the dinosaurs.

36 **Some reptiles began to look very much like mammals.** *Cynognathus* was as big as a large dog, and instead of scaly skin it had fur. It belonged to a group of reptiles called therapsids. Around 220 million years ago, some types of small therapsids were evolving into the first mammals.

◀ The jaws of *Cynognathus* were so powerful they could bite through bone. Its name means 'dog jaw'.

Living with the dinosaurs

37 **Some reptiles were as big and fierce as dinosaurs – but they lived in the sea.** One of these was *Mosasaurus*. It grew up to 10 metres in length and may have weighed 10 tonnes, far bigger than today's great white shark.

38 **One sea reptile had teeth the size of saucers!** The huge, round, flat teeth of *Placodus* were more than 10 centimetres across. It used them to crush shellfish and sea urchins. *Placodus* was 2 metres long and lived at the same time as the first dinosaurs, about 230 million years ago.

I DON'T BELIEVE IT!
Fossils of *Mosasaurus* were found in the same place over 200 years apart! The first was found in a quarry in the Netherlands in 1780. The second was found in the same place in 1998.

▼ *Mosasaurus* was a huge sea reptile. It had razor-sharp teeth and could swim with speed to catch its prey.

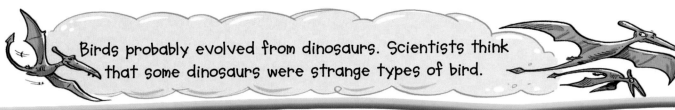

▼ *Archaeopteryx* had a long bony tail, unlike modern birds, which have no bones in their tails.

39

Fossils of the first bird were mistaken for a dinosaur. *Archaeopteryx* lived in Europe about 155 million years ago. Some of its fossils look very similar to the fossils of small dinosaurs. So *Archaeopteryx* was thought to be a dinosaur, until scientists saw the faint shape of its feathers and realized it was a bird.

40

Soon there were many kinds of birds flying above the dinosaurs. *Confuciusornis* was about 60 centimetres long and lived in what is now China, 120 million years ago. It had a backwards-pointing big toe on each foot, which suggests it climbed through the trees. It is also the earliest-known bird to have a true beak.

▲ Fossils of *Confuciusornis* have been found in China. It is named after the famous Chinese wise man, Confucius.

41

Mammals lived at the same time as dinosaurs. These animals have warm blood, and fur or hair, unlike a reptile's scaly skin. *Megazostrodon* was the earliest mammal known to scientists. It lived in southern Africa about 215 million years ago – only 15 million years or so after the dinosaurs began life on Earth. It was just 12 centimetres long, and probably hunted insects.

▼ *Megazostrodon* probably came out at night to hunt for its insect prey. It looked a little like a modern-day shrew.

In and over the sea

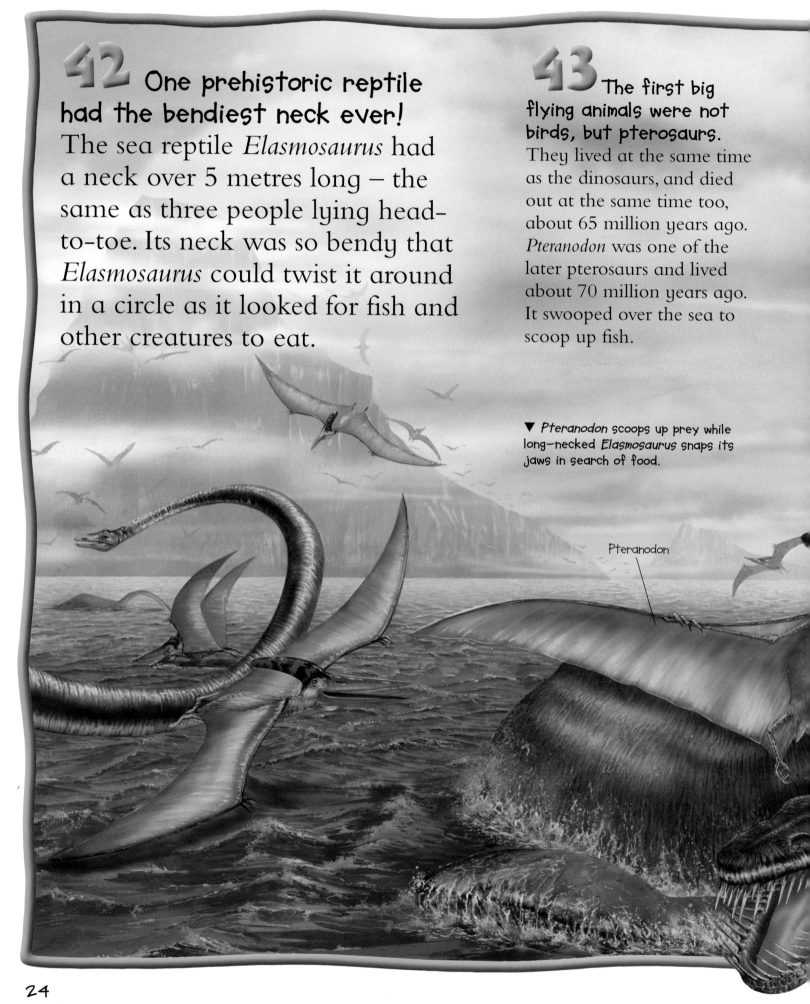

42 One prehistoric reptile had the bendiest neck ever! The sea reptile *Elasmosaurus* had a neck over 5 metres long – the same as three people lying head-to-toe. Its neck was so bendy that *Elasmosaurus* could twist it around in a circle as it looked for fish and other creatures to eat.

43 The first big flying animals were not birds, but pterosaurs. They lived at the same time as the dinosaurs, and died out at the same time too, about 65 million years ago. *Pteranodon* was one of the later pterosaurs and lived about 70 million years ago. It swooped over the sea to scoop up fish.

▼ *Pteranodon* scoops up prey while long-necked *Elasmosaurus* snaps its jaws in search of food.

Pteranodon

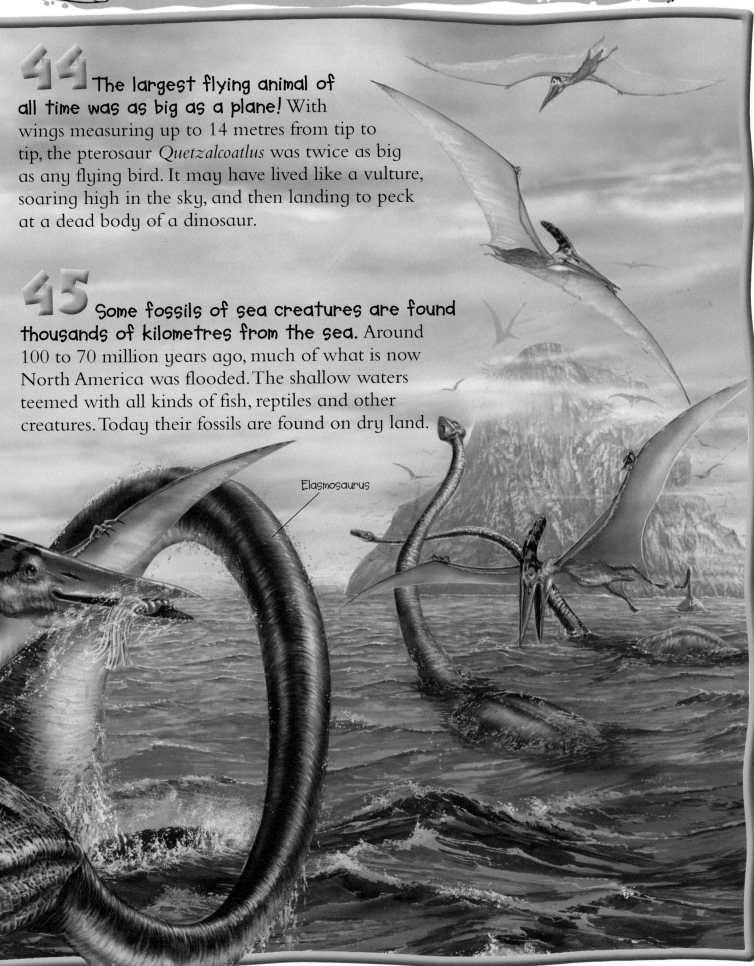

44 **The largest flying animal of all time was as big as a plane!** With wings measuring up to 14 metres from tip to tip, the pterosaur *Quetzalcoatlus* was twice as big as any flying bird. It may have lived like a vulture, soaring high in the sky, and then landing to peck at a dead body of a dinosaur.

45 **Some fossils of sea creatures are found thousands of kilometres from the sea.** Around 100 to 70 million years ago, much of what is now North America was flooded. The shallow waters teemed with all kinds of fish, reptiles and other creatures. Today their fossils are found on dry land.

Elasmosaurus

After the dinosaurs

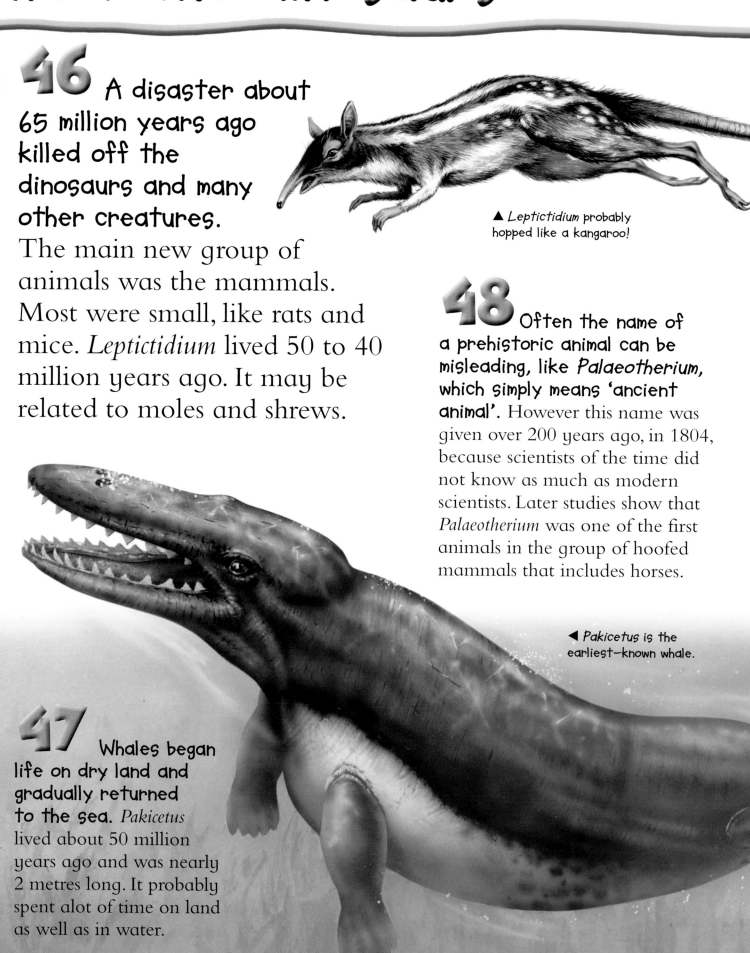

46 A disaster about 65 million years ago killed off the dinosaurs and many other creatures. The main new group of animals was the mammals. Most were small, like rats and mice. *Leptictidium* lived 50 to 40 million years ago. It may be related to moles and shrews.

▲ *Leptictidium* probably hopped like a kangaroo!

48 Often the name of a prehistoric animal can be misleading, like *Palaeotherium*, which simply means 'ancient animal'. However this name was given over 200 years ago, in 1804, because scientists of the time did not know as much as modern scientists. Later studies show that *Palaeotherium* was one of the first animals in the group of hoofed mammals that includes horses.

◀ *Pakicetus* is the earliest-known whale.

47 Whales began life on dry land and gradually returned to the sea. *Pakicetus* lived about 50 million years ago and was nearly 2 metres long. It probably spent alot of time on land as well as in water.

Mammals began to grow larger and become more numerous after the dinosaurs had died out.

▼ A mother *Uintatherium* and her baby. This strange-looking creature was the largest land animal of its time. Its head was covered in horns and it had small tusks.

49 Around 40 million years ago, the largest animal walking the Earth was *Uintatherium*. This plant eater was over 3 metres long and nearly 2 metres tall at the shoulder – about the same size as a cow. Its fossils were found near the Uinta River in Colorado, USA. *Uintatherium* is thought to be a cousin of horses and elephants.

50 An animal's looks can be misleading. *Patriofelis* means 'father of the cats'. It lived 45 million years ago and was named because scientists thought it looked like an early cat. Later they realized that it merely looked like a cat. It was really a member of an extinct group of hunting animals called creodonts.

QUIZ
1. What does the name *Patriofelis* mean?
2. How long was *Pakicetus*?
3. In what year were *Palaeotherium* fossils found?
4. How tall was *Uintatherium*?
5. When did dinosaurs die out and mammals start to take over?

Answers:
1. 'Father of the cats'
2. About 2 metres 3. 1804
4. Almost 2 metres tall at the shoulder
5. 65 million years ago

As the world cooled down

51 Before the world started to cool 30 million years ago, palm trees grew almost everywhere – but they became rare. These trees had thrived in warm, wet conditions. But as Earth cooled, other plants took over, such as magnolias, pines, oaks and birch. These changes meant that animals changed too.

▼ *Brontotherium* was somewhere in size between a rhino and an elephant. Males used the Y–shaped horn on their snouts in fighting competitions.

52 *Pyrotherium* means 'fire beast', but not because this plant eater could walk through fire. Its fossils were found in layers of ash from an ancient volcano in Argentina, South America. The volcano probably erupted, and its fumes and ash suffocated and burned all the animals nearby. *Pyrotherium* was about as big as a cow and looked like a combination of a pig and a short-tusked elephant.

53 Many prehistoric animals have exciting names – *Brontotherium* means 'thunder beast'. Where the fossils of *Brontotherium* were found in North America, local people thought they were bones of the gods. They thought that these gods rode chariots across the sky and started thunderstorms, which led to the animal's name.

54 **Andrewsarchus was a real big-head!** At one metre long, it had the biggest head of any hunting mammal on land, and its strong jaws were filled with sharp, pointed teeth. Its whole body was bigger than a tiger of today. *Andrewsarchus* probably lived like a hyena, crunching up bones and gristle from dead animals. Yet it belonged to a mammal group that was mostly plant eaters. It lived 30 million years ago in what is now the deserts of Mongolia, Asia.

▲ *Andrewsarchus* was the biggest meat-eating land animal ever to have lived.

QUIZ
1. What does *Brontotherium* mean?
2. What does *Pyrotherium* mean?
3. How long was the head of *Andrewsarchus*?
4. Where did *Arsinoitherium* live?

Answers:
1. 'Thunder beast' 2. 'Fire beast' 3. One metre 4. Northern Africa

▲ The horns on *Arsinoitherium's* head were hollow and may have been used to make mating calls.

55 **Some animals had horns as tall as people!** *Arsinoitherium's* two massive horns looked like powerful weapons – but they were light, fragile and made of very thin bone. This plant eater lived in northern Africa about 35 million years ago. It was almost as big as an elephant and may have been an ancient cousin of the elephant group.

What fossils tell us

56 Fossils are the remains of animals or plants that have been preserved in rock. Usually only the hard parts of an animal, such as teeth or bones, are preserved in this way. Trilobites had a tough, outer skeleton so usually only this part of their body is found as a fossil. Scientists use the fossil to try to create a picture of how the soft parts, such as muscles and organs, may have looked.

▲ By examining trilobite fossils, scientists were able to tell that this animal could see in all directions.

▼ Some early humans are known only from their fossil footprints, not from fossils of their bones. These footprints were discovered in 1978 in Tanzania, Africa.

57 Some fossils are known as trace fossils. These are not fossilized parts of an animal's body, such as bones, but preserved marks left behind by the animal, such as footprints or droppings. By studying the fossilized footprints of an extinct animal, scientists can discover how it walked, how fast it could move and whether it lived alone or in groups.

It is actually very rare for an animal to be fossilized. Most animals rot away or are eaten after they die.

58
On rare occasions the softer parts of an animal may be preserved as well as the hard parts. Insects may become trapped in sticky sap oozing from pine trees. This sap may then become fossilized as amber, with the insect caught inside. Scientists have found hundreds of insects, spiders and other small creatures perfectly preserved in this way.

▲ Amber spider fossils show that spiders have changed little over the last 30 million years.

QUIZ
1. What is a fossil?
2. What could scientists tell from trilobite fossils?
3. What is amber?
4. What animals did Archaeopteryx look like?

Answers:
1. Remains of animals or plants preserved in rock 2. That they could see in all directions 3. Fossil tree sap 4. A bird and a dinosaur

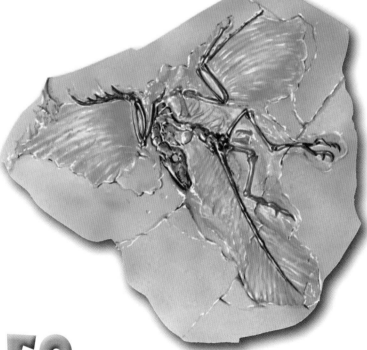

◄ Some fossils of *Archaeopteryx* are so well preserved that even the feathers can be seen.

59
One of the most important and valuable fossils ever found was of *Archaeopteryx*, in Germany in 1860. The fossil is about 150 million years old and shows a creature that looked part dinosaur and part bird. It had the feathers and wings of a bird, but the teeth and bony tail of a dinosaur. This shows that birds probably evolved from a type of dinosaur.

60
The importance of some fossils can be misunderstood. *Acanthostega* was one of the very earliest amphibian fossils ever found. However, the man who found the fossil was not an expert on amphibians. When his expedition returned from Greenland, the fossil was put in a drawer at a museum. It was not until over 30 years later that an expert on amphibians happened to see the fossil and realized how important it was.

Prehistoric prowlers

61 Some animals probably ate just about anything. Entelodonts were piglike animals that lived about 25 million years ago. *Dinohyus* was one of the largest entelodonts. Its teeth were sharp and strong, and it had powerful jaw muscles. It ate almost anything from leaves, roots and seeds, to small animals.

62 Some predators (hunting animals) walked on tiptoe but others were flat-footed. Most mammal predators, such as cats and dogs, walk on the ends of their toes. This helps them to run faster. *Daphoenodon* walked on flat feet, like a bear. It is often called a 'bear-dog' as it looked like a dog but walked like a bear.

▼ *Dinohyus* lived in North America and grew to be about 3 metres long. Its powerful neck muscles and large canine teeth suggest it could have broken bones and eaten flesh.

63

Fossils can show if predators hunted by day or at night. *Plesictis* was 75 centimetres long and its fossils show it had large sockets (spaces) for its eyes. This means that it probably hunted at night. It also had sharp claws and a long tail, so it probably scampered through trees hunting birds and insects, gripping with its claws and balancing with its tail.

64

Some predators have changed little over millions of years. *Potamotherium* was an early otter and lived in Europe, 23 million years ago. It looked almost like the otters of today. Its shape was so well-suited to hunting fish in streams that it has hardly changed.

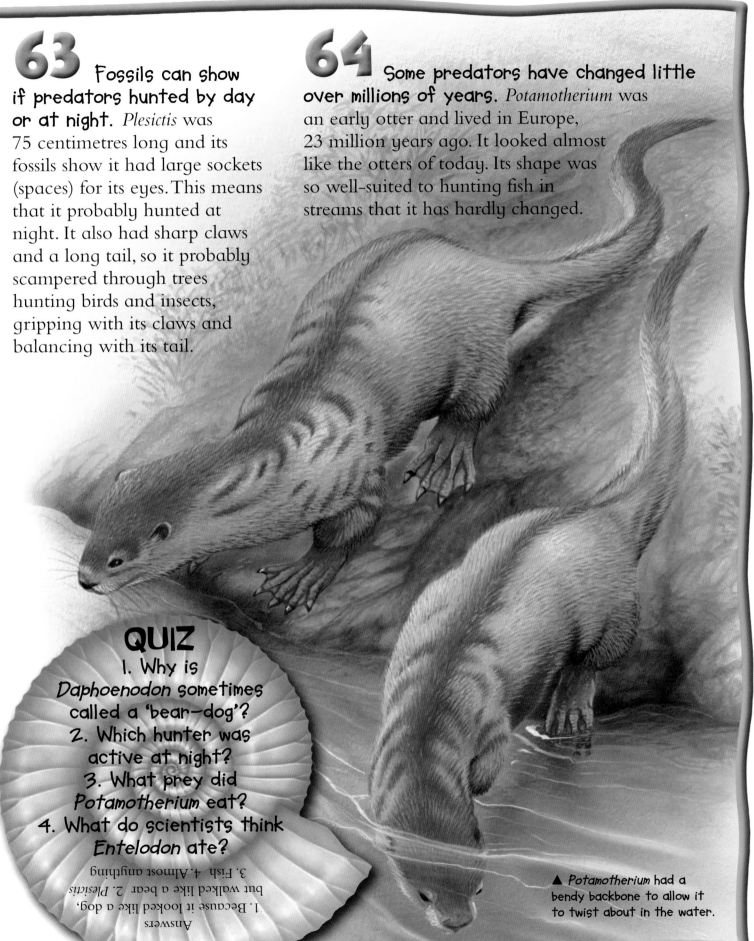

▲ *Potamotherium* had a bendy backbone to allow it to twist about in the water.

QUIZ
1. Why is *Daphoenodon* sometimes called a 'bear-dog'?
2. Which hunter was active at night?
3. What prey did *Potamotherium* eat?
4. What do scientists think *Entelodon* ate?

Answers
1. Because it looked like a dog, but walked like a bear 2. *Plesictis* 3. Fish 4. Almost anything

Amazing ancient elephants

65 **The first elephant had tiny tusks and almost no trunk.** *Moeritherium* lived in northern Africa about 36 million years ago. It stood just 60 centimetres tall and may have weighed around 20 kilograms – about the size of a large pet dog.

I DON'T BELIEVE IT!

The tusks of *Anancus* were over 4 metres long – almost as long as the animal itself.

▶ Woolly mammoths had coats of shaggy hair. This hair kept their warm inner fur dry and waterproof in the freezing conditions of the ice age.

66 **Some elephants were very hairy.** The woolly mammoth was covered in thick, long dense hair to keep out the cold of the ice age. It was larger than a modern elephant and was probably hunted by early people. The last woolly mammoths may have died out less than 10,000 years ago.

67 **One elephant had tusks like shovels.** *Platybelodon* lived about nine million years ago in Europe, Asia and Africa. Its lower tusks were shaped like broad, flat shovels. Perhaps it used them to scoop up water plants to eat.

68 **Some elephants had four tusks.** *Tetralophodon* lived about eight million years ago and stood 3 metres tall. Its fossils have been found in Europe, Asia, Africa and America, so it was a very widespread and successful animal.

69 **The biggest elephant was the Columbian mammoth.** It stood 4 metres tall and may have weighed over 10 tonnes – twice as much as most elephants today. It lived on the grasslands of southern North America.

▼ The Columbian mammoth had tusks that twisted into curved, spiral shapes.

70 **Elephants were more varied and common long ago, than they are today.** *Anancus* roamed Europe and Asia two million years ago. Like modern elephants, it used its trunk to pull leaves from branches and its tusks to dig up roots. However most kinds of prehistoric elephants died out. Only two kinds survive today, in Africa and Asia.

Animals with hooves

71 **The first horse was hardly larger than a pet cat.** *Hyracotherium* lived in Europe, Asia and North America about 50 million years ago. It was only 20 centimetres tall and lived in woods and forests.

▼ *Hyracotherium* is sometimes called *Eohippus*, which means 'dawn horse'. It had a short neck, slender legs and a long tail.

72 **Early horses did not eat grass – because there wasn't any.** Grasses and open plains did not appear on Earth until 25 million years ago. Then early horses moved onto them, started to eat grass, and gradually became bigger.

73 **Over millions of years, horses gradually lost their toes!** The very first horses had five toes per foot, each ending in a small nail-like hoof. *Hyracotherium* had four toes on each front foot and three on each back foot. Later, *Mesohippus*, which was as big as a labrador dog, had three toes on each foot. Today's horses have just one toe on each foot, which ends in a large hoof.

74 Some prehistoric camels had horns. *Synthetoceras* had a pair of horns at the top of its head, and also an extraordinary Y-shaped horn growing from its nose. It probably used these horns to fight enemies and also to show off to others of its kind at breeding time.

▶ The amazing nose horn of *Synthetoceras* was present only on male animals.

◀ *Megaloceros* may have stored food for the winter in the form of fat in a hump on its shoulder.

HORSE RACE

You will need:
stiff card   crayons
scissors   string
about 4 metres long

On the card, draw a picture of *Hyracotherium*. Colour it in and cut it out. Make a hole in the middle, about 2 centimetres from the top. Thread the string through the hole and tie one end to a piece of furniture. Pull the string tight, then flick it with a finger to make *Hyracotherium* move along!

75 Some prehistoric deer had antlers as big as a person! *Megaloceros* means 'big deer' and it was as big as today's biggest deer, the moose. But its antlers were even bigger, measuring almost 4 metres from tip to tip. *Megaloceros* may have survived in some parts of Europe until as little as 3000 years ago.

Cats, dogs and bears

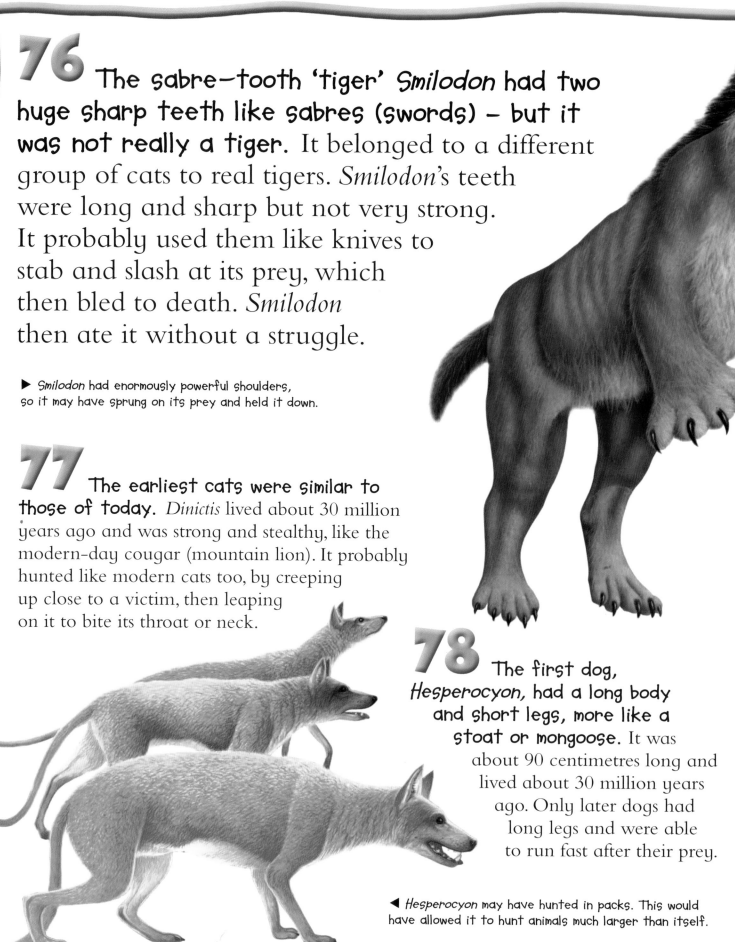

76 The sabre-tooth 'tiger' *Smilodon* had two huge sharp teeth like sabres (swords) – but it was not really a tiger. It belonged to a different group of cats to real tigers. *Smilodon*'s teeth were long and sharp but not very strong. It probably used them like knives to stab and slash at its prey, which then bled to death. *Smilodon* then ate it without a struggle.

▶ *Smilodon* had enormously powerful shoulders, so it may have sprung on its prey and held it down.

77 The earliest cats were similar to those of today. *Dinictis* lived about 30 million years ago and was strong and stealthy, like the modern-day cougar (mountain lion). It probably hunted like modern cats too, by creeping up close to a victim, then leaping on it to bite its throat or neck.

78 The first dog, *Hesperocyon*, had a long body and short legs, more like a stoat or mongoose. It was about 90 centimetres long and lived about 30 million years ago. Only later dogs had long legs and were able to run fast after their prey.

◀ *Hesperocyon* may have hunted in packs. This would have allowed it to hunt animals much larger than itself.

Nearly all meat-eating mammals alive today belong to the animal group Carnivora.

79 The sabre-tooth 'cat' *Thylacosmilus* was not even a real cat! It had a cat-shaped head, body, legs and tail. Yet it was a marsupial – a cousin of kangaroos and koalas. It lived in South America four million years ago.

80 Sea lions did not develop from lions – but from dogs. *Allodesmus* was an early type of sea lion and lived about 13 million years ago. It had strong flippers for fast swimming. Its fossil bones show that it came originally from the dog group.

I DON'T BELIEVE IT!

Even if global warming continues, the world will not be as hot as it was 35 million years ago.

◀ Early humans had to face many natural dangers, such as cave bears.

81 Early people hunted cave bears, and cave bears hunted early people! The huge cave bear of the Ice Age was as big as today's grizzly bear. Humans called Neanderthals hunted them and used their bones and teeth as ornaments. The bears hunted people too, and left their bones in caves.

Prehistoric giants

82 **The largest flying bird ever was as big as a small plane!** *Argentavis* was twice the size of any flying bird today. Its wings measured 7 metres from tip to tip. It was a huge vulture that fed on the dead bodies of other creatures, tearing off their flesh with its powerful hooked beak.

▼ *Argentavis* lived about seven million years ago in South America.

83 **Some birds were even bigger than** *Argentavis*, **but they could not fly – and they were deadly hunters.** In South America about one million years ago, *Titanis* grew to 3 metres tall. It raced after its prey, which it tore apart with its huge, hooked beak.

84 **A type of prehistoric kangaroo,** *Procoptodon*, **was twice as big as those of today.** Yet it could bound along as fast as a racehorse. Like kangaroos of today, it was a marsupial, carrying its baby in a pouch. It lived in Australia.

◄ *Titanis* was a monstrous hunting bird that chased after mammals such as this early horse, in South America.

The largest mammal that ever lived is still alive today – the enormous blue whale.

85 The largest land mammal ever to have lived was a type of rhino – without a nose horn.
Paraceratherium was far bigger than an elephant, at 8 metres long and 6 metres tall at the shoulder. It weighed over 15 tonnes – more than three elephants. This giant creature lived in Asia about 30 million years ago and was a peaceful plant eater.

I DON'T BELIEVE IT!
Giant marsupials may have started stories of the 'Bunyip', a mythical Australian animal.

▲ The huge *Paraceratherium* fed by browsing on trees, stripping off the leaves. Even though it was so big and heavy, *Paraceratherium* had long legs, which means it was probably capable of running.

A giant island

86 For almost 50 million years, South America was like a giant island – with many strange animals that were found nowhere else. Until three million years ago, South America was separated from North America by an ocean. On islands, animals can evolve into unusual kinds found nowhere else in the world.

87 Elephants were not the only animals with trunks! *Macrauchenia* lived in South America about 100,000 years ago. It was about the size of a camel and probably had a trunk to gather leaves to eat. It was not a type of elephant, but a distant cousin of horses and rhinos.

Macrauchenia

▶ South America was once separated from North America. This meant that certain animals that survived there did not live anywhere else in the world.

88 When South America joined North America, many kinds of prehistoric animals died out. In particular, animals from North America spread south. They were better at surviving than the South American creatures, and they gradually took over.

89 One South American creature that has died out was the giant sloth, *Megatherium*. It was a cousin of the smaller sloths that live in trees today – but it was far too big to climb trees. At 6 metres long and 3 tonnes in weight, it was the size of an elephant! It may have died out only in the last few thousand years.

90 Armadillos were once nearly as big as tanks! *Glyptodon* was almost 4 metres long and covered in a thick dome of bony armour. It lived in South America until about 10,000 years ago. Today, armadillos are quite small, but they are still covered in bony plates for protection.

Megatherium

Glyptodon

I DON'T BELIEVE IT!
The armadillo is a South American animal that lives in North America, too. Over the past 100 years, it has spread north at a rate of one kilometre every ten years.

43

Our prehistoric relations

91 Monkeys, apes and humans first appeared over 50 million years ago – the first kinds looked like squirrels. This group is called the primates. *Plesiadapis* was one of the first primates. It lived 55 million years ago in Europe and North America.

◀ *Plesiadapis* had claws on its fingers and toes, unlike monkeys and apes, which had nails.

92 Early apes walked on all fours. About 20 million years ago, *Dryopithecus* lived in Europe and Asia. It used its arms and legs to climb trees. When it came down to the ground, it walked on all fours. It was 60 centimetres long and ate fruit and leaves.

▶ The early ape *Dryopithecus* walked flat on its feet, unlike other apes, which walked on their knuckles.

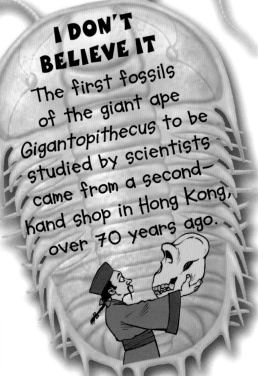

I DON'T BELIEVE IT

The first fossils of the giant ape *Gigantopithecus* to be studied by scientists came from a second-hand shop in Hong Kong, over 70 years ago.

Walking on two legs meant that *Ardipithecus* was free to carry things such as food or babies.

▼ The need to see longer distances on grasslands may have caused the first apes to walk on two legs.

93 Some kinds of apes may have walked on their two back legs, like us. About 4.5 million years ago *Ardipithecus* lived in Africa. Only a few of its fossils have been found. However, experts think it may have walked upright on its back legs. It could have made the first steps in the change, or evolution, from apes to humans.

94 One prehistoric ape was a real giant – over 3 metres tall! Its name, *Gigantopithecus*, means 'giant ape'. It was much larger than today's biggest ape, the gorilla, which grows to 2 metres tall. *Gigantopithecus* probably ate roots and seeds, and may have hunted small animals such as birds, rats and lizards.

▶ The enormous *Gigantopithecus* could probably stand on its hind legs to reach food.

95 Scientists work out which animals are our closest cousins partly from fossils – and also from chemicals. The chemical called DNA contains genes, which are instructions for how living things grow and work. The living animals with DNA most similar to ours are the great apes, chimpanzees and gorillas, both from Africa. So our ancient cousins were probably apes like them. The orang-utan, from Southeast Asia, is less similar.

The first humans

▼ *Australopithecus* walked upright. It spent most of its days searching for food.

96 Our early prehistoric cousins were much smaller than us. One kind was called *Australopithecus afarensis*, meaning 'southern ape from Afar', because its fossils come from the Afar region of East Africa. It was just over one metre tall, lived over three million years ago, and looked part human and part ape.

▶ *Homo erectus* was the first living creature to use fire for cooking and warmth.

97 Very early kinds of humans lived almost two million years ago. They were called *Homo erectus*, which means 'upright human', and they were as tall as us. These first humans spread from Africa, across Asia, and into Europe. However, they all died out about 200,000 years ago.

98 From one million years ago early people made tools out of stone – they had not invented metal. They chipped rocks like flint to form a sharp, cutting edge, and shaped stones into knives, scrapers, or axes. Stone tools have been found with the bones of animals that were cut up for food, along with the ashes of fires used for cooking – and the bones of the people themselves.

99 **Some prehistoric animals were domesticated (tamed) to become the first farm animals.** This began around 15,000 years ago. For example, fierce aurochs, a type of wild cow, were gradually bred over time to become quiet, calm animals. They provided people with food and clothing.

▶ The Flores humans probably used stone tools to hunt animals such as the pygmy elephant.

100 **We are still discovering surprises about prehistoric life.** In 2004, scientists found the bones and tools of tiny humans, less than one metre tall, on the island of Flores in Southeast Asia. Their remains are from over 90,000 to less than 15,000 years old. No one knew they existed. In the future we may discover more amazing finds from the past.

QUIZ
1. Were prehistoric humans big or small?
2. What were the first tools made from?
3. When were animals first domesticated?
4. What was discovered on the island of Flores?

Answers:
1. Small 2. Stone 3. 15,000 years ago
4. Flores man

Index